7 Ways to Get Energy

by Linda Yoshizawa

 HOUGHTON MIFFLIN   BOSTON

All living things need energy. Energy lets us move and grow. It lets us do the things we want to do. Energy comes from the Sun.

Plants get energy from the Sun. They also need water, air, and other things from the soil. Plants use sunlight to make their own food.

Animals do not make their own food.
Some animals eat only plants. That's where they
get their energy.

Some animals eat other animals.
These animals get energy by eating the meat
of other animals.

Bears get energy in many ways. They eat both plants and animals. Bears eat fish, but they also eat berries and other fruits, nuts, honey, mushrooms, and vegetables. Sometimes they will eat frogs, bees, and small animals.

People are animals too. People get energy from eating plants and animals. A hamburger comes from an animal—a cow. Salad comes from plants—lettuce and carrots.

Plants and animals are all linked in a chain we call a food chain. Here is an example of a food chain. The sun helps the corn make its own food. The chicken eats the corn. And people eat the meat from the chicken.